# DETROIT
# DETROIT

# DETROIT DETROIT

## ANNA VITALE

ROOF BOOKS
NEW YORK

ISBN: 978-1-931824-69-9
Library of Congress Control Number: 2017932309

Acknowledgments

An earlier version of "In School" was published in *The Brooklyn Rail*. "We Built This City" was first published in *Fanzine*. "Street View Lyric" was originally published as a video by *Gauss PDF*. This writing benefitted from many conversations with many people and I'm grateful to everyone, but in particular: Anselm Berrigan, Brandon Brown, Marie Buck, River Anita Bullock, Julia Dauer, Thom Donovan, Jordan Dunn, Ren Evans, Brad Flis, Lewis Freedman, Andy Gricevich, Rob Halpern, Lenora Hanson, Roberto Harrison, Carla Harryman, Jeremy Hoevenaar, Josef Kaplan, Holly Melgard, Ken Mikolowski, Judah Rubin, Rebecca Couch Steffy, Cassandra Troyan, Dana Ward, Brian Whitener, and Matvei Yankelevich.

NEW YORK STATE OF OPPORTUNITY | Council on the Arts — This book is made possible, in part, by the New York State Council on the Arts with the support of Governor Andrew Cuomo and the New York State Legislature.

Roof Books
are published by
Segue Foundation
300 Bowery, New York, NY 10012
seguefoundation.com

Roof Books
are distributed by
Small Press Distribution
1341 Seventh Street
Berkeley, CA. 94710-1403
800-869-7553 or spdbooks.org

*This book is dedicated to*
Casey Girardin (1981-2015)
&
Martha Guttshall (1955-1965)

# Contents

Uh Uh
    Uh Uh
    Detroit Dream
    Dedication
    Renaissance

Just hold on, we're going home
                    —Drake

Having been born October 7, my nature
was to listen to everybody, to be sensitive
to, and look at, everything. But my
tendency, body and mind, is to make it.
To get there, from anywhere, going
wherever, always. By the time this book
appears, I will be even blacker.
                    —Amiri Baraka, *Home: Social Essays*


                    Going

                    Social
                    Essays

                    Going
                    Going

                    Just Hold On,
                    We're Going [        ]

                    Social
                    Essays

                    Going
                    Going

                    Just Hold On,
                    We're Going [        ]

Uh uh
Uh uh

Going
Going

Social
Essays

Uh uh
Uh uh

Going
Going

Just Hold On,
We're Going [    ]

Going
Going

Just Hold On,

Going

Social
Essays

Uh uh
Uh uh

*

Having been
Born going

His nature was
To be sensitive
To listen

*

I got
My eyes
On [      ]

To get
Over to
Make it

You left
Your
Mark to

Get to
Your
Mark

Essays
Will to

Be
Black

*

Just hold on
We're going [      ]

Uh uh
Uh uh

Social
Essays

Uh uh
Uh uh

Cuz yr a
good [      ]

And you
know

My tendency
to make

Cuz yr
a good

[     ] and
you know

My tendency is
to make

I know
exactly who

You could
[     ]

Just Hold On

To Flaunt
This Py-
Re Where
Pier

Stretches
White Body
The Bo-
Dy My Bo-
Dy of Witch-
Es What Bo-
Dy What
Scatt-
Ered Girl-
Y Stor-
Y Folded
And Fold-
Ed Bids
Herd-
Ed Chipp-
Ed Wont to
Make
Smok-
Ed Won't
Have Touch-
Ed Mind-
Ed Mouth-
Ed Re-
Fused

Going
[     ]

Come
Back
Blacker

But eve-
n black-
er, right eve-
n black-

er, right eve-
n black-
er, eh

Going
[     ]

Come
Black

Just
hold

Prove
it

*

Scars
Cars
Bars on
Windows
Reams
Draped on
Sides
Hide
Beams
Beams and
Shadows
The Hearts
of Me-
Mes
So what
When
We tear
Tear apart

A sun
Dead
Under
Us by uh
Uh Cross
Be
Billie
Uh Uh
Shadow

Who knows
That best
Who knows
That suffering

*

Scars
Cars
Bars on
Windows
This
Skin
Shack
That can't
Get

Uh to
Live to
Go to

Whose
[      ]

This
[      ]

Whose
[     ]

Is
Race
Streets
Place
Subtle
Slash
Toy
Mic
Mic
Whose
Register

The Owners
Versus Those
Who Moan
The Take-Away

And There Is
a Storm that
Rolls in from the
Side of His Eye

Fight for
His Corner

Fight for
My

Scars
Cars Bars
Prove
It

\*

Listen to
Tendency to
Get to
Black to
Adjust
White
Out

We were on Longacre and Pascal was there and another person a girl was there and I don't know I don't know why we were there Bobby J's face was so nice I uh was saying goodbye to him and um he was taking a shower and I had to knock on the door and I wanted I wanted to say goodbye so um I poked my head into the into the bathroom and I was knocking and knocking and I was saying you know Bobby we're leaving uh and Pascal was in the hallway and uh Bobby J got out of the shower uh naked and of course I looked at his penis but I didn't I don't know he was just being flirty really but there was a lot of uh desire between us and he said well come on in and he was gesturing towards like I should get in the shower with him and I said no no we're leaving and he said well he wanted me to stay and uh he we kissed each other a lot but um like on the cheek sort of European uh you know style and he clearly it was hard it was hard to say no I had a fantasy of going back um and and being with him and I was but I was trying to get him to be quiet about uh the desire um but I I grabbed his face at some point and I said oh my god I'm so glad that you're okay I saw pictures of you on facebook and you were so beat up you had scars all over your face and tattoos all over your body gang tattoos all over your body and it was clear you'd survived fights but I didn't think that you were okay and and I had my hands against his cheeks and his yeah his face in my hands and I said I'm so I'm just so glad that you're ok

Ten years ago I wrote a story about Bobby J and called him Justin Shine. The story is called The Death of Justin Shine. "The Death of Justin Shine." Justin Shine died on a Friday morning. Sandy called to tell me. The sky was blue. It was summer. Summers in Detroit were the best. We filled the streets. Too big to walk on the sidewalk meant for couples with children or dogs. Flowers wilted as we walked by. Justin Shine worked at the Paul Store. I was painting my nails and having trouble because I'm not left-handed when Sandy called. *Hello. Hi. Hi. Do you know that Justin Shine died? Oh my god, when? This morning. What happened? I don't know. Oh. Oh.* He was wearing a blue and black Fila jacket. I changed positions on the bed so I could lie down and stare blankly through the sky.

We were we were on Longacre and it seemed very dangerous we also seemed different because I was worried that we'd get jumped white kids with luggage and laptops and we didn't belong and I was I was trying to take a blanket that Bobby had made that had something to do with Detroit uh but I couldn't figure out which blanket was the one that I had been using all week and the one that I wanted um I ended up taking a t-shirt that he'd made instead and it said something about your feet in academia it was funny the sentiment was like I guess well now that I'm saying it I don't know uh it's embarrassing it was a green shirt and I think the sentiment was something silly like your feet in academia your heart in Detroit but I don't think that's that's not what it said it was more complicated um there was text that was crossed out and there was text that was printed on the shirt and there was text that was written on the shirt there was a picture uh on the shirt it had a picture of a pair of legs tangled up at the edge of a curb like hanging off the curb like it was really big and the body's legs were really small um there were blankets on which he'd printed crossword puzzles too uh but those weren't the blankets that I wanted there was a blanket with stripes that had to do with Detroit that I wanted I was telling somebody at a store that there had always been a store there and I was gesturing to Serv-U-Well but I was calling it Gettysburg Address I was saying there's always been a store there it's Gettysburg Gettysburg Address and then I said and next to that there's always been a shitty bakery and it's Star Bakery

I was uh giving a speech about permanence um I mean I was I'm I call it permanence cuz I was just saying the what buildings had always been there or what and what businesses had always been in those buildings and I don't know who I was talking to but it was very inspired

We were on a bus it was going down Longacre the bus went around parked cars but we were going towards Warren and the bus went around parked cars that were headed that that were that were directed towards Whitlock and so that meant that the bus went that the bus fit between the space of a car and the space of a curb and that the doorside to the curb we weren't doorside at the curb uh the bus fit between a cuh—like two inches between the car and the curb and people went around the bus to get on and everyone was oohing and ahhing that we fit in that tiny spot um and didn't hit any cars and then lots of people got on the bus well the feeling in the dream even though the neighborhood is dangerous and I'm scared we're gonna get jumped and I feel especially marked because I think we're all grad students and and Pascal is the man in the group you know doesn't look like he's gonna be able to fight anyone if they come after us uh I know that he's jealous of my relationship with Bobby but I also try to reject Bobby even though I feel he's better for me in some ways but I don't want to hurt Pascal and I also realize that Bobby's part of the past um I want to be near him again so I am trying to send him a text message to say that does he want to get together and do homework I can do my Old English or maybe it's German uh I want to make an effort to pay attention to him and not uh and not dreams about Detroit

I know this might sound dumb, but I think of you almost every time I think. To me, you represent even though you haven't been elected. When I think of being white or being a woman, I remember the prohibitions in place regarding our friendship, so we have had a secret friendship, one which I'm dying to share. This secret comes back, it's recursive. It's like what it's like to date, to hold hands, to be found in bed together is tied up with prohibition. It's like what it's like is being tied up by rules we didn't make. When you find this note, please think of it like the child we have, proof that we break when we can only remember what was wished for. I will send you the book this note is in. I will send you every book I write.

Heading into the army, you know what you're giving up, but what will it feel like: your body and your relationship to bodies, growing up to be in the service of others, to have your friend's back, to defend our neighborhood. I miss our army. I am ashamed of not having been asked to attend this school where you show up every day and are asked to do the impossible and everyone agrees about the impossibility and yet still behaves as if it's achievable. Something about recruitment because I want you. I do not think I am supposed to. My attachment to our mannerisms is overboard. It swells. My attachment is felt through our attachments, gold husks, black shells, white teeth, the adherent of song, morphology, the usu. I touch you. My hand slips between the band of your briefs and your stomach. Your patience sticks. First hand, first love, we will find ourselves in hell. I think of the violence we are born with and how "I" was civilized. When you unbutton my shirt, you always like my red bra. You say I have a body, which means a nice body, but you don't say "nice," you just say "body."

There were fish in a jar. There was water in the fridge in a big, big container and I was trying to do something with the water. I don't know what. And then I looked in the fridge and fish had begun to form themselves in the water in the jar in the fridge. And I thought at first they were bean sprouts. They looked like the size of white bean sprouts and I wasn't sure how those would have gotten in there. Maybe I hadn't washed out the jar well enough maybe somebody thought it would be funny to put bean sprouts in my jug of water. And then I saw one move and I didn't think that it could move and so it must be that the water's moving but then the other ones moved and also seemed to have tongues that came out of what looked like heads and they were swimming around and sticking their tongues out like snakes and I suppose they got big and bigger and bigger pretty quickly and they were forming a team a body uh that seemed dangerous in this big big jug of water in the fridge that obviously could not be used for anything now and the only trick was how to dispose of it without being attacked. And there was someone in the bathroom. Someone getting ready in the bathroom. There were lots of clothes on the floor and I the jug had a top and at one point the jug had a very large mouth to it rather than a small um spouty-like top and the large mouth was more like the mouth of a jar the rest of the size of the vessel um not really narrowing at the top that's what I'm trying to explain so this wide mouth at the top was the first kind of top this jug had but the top to the jug itself was very low into the body of the vessel and so I was going to have to reach far down into it in order to unscrew the top which I felt like put me in more danger since I was already going into something um and not just being able to be on the surface and unscrew this tiny cap but then when I got to the toilet I was gonna I had decided the best thing to do with these things is to flush them down the toilet and flush all this water down the toilet because it will just go. When I got to the toilet the mouth was very small at the top and I couldn't even think about how these fish were gonna get out and then all the water seemed kind of frozen so when I tried to pour the water into the toilet from this tiny little tiny little spout it didn't seem like it was gonna come out because so much of it was frozen except these weird tadpole fish eel nasty bean sprout aqua bodies which were still alive but then I dumped it somehow and missed the toilet and it was on the floor which meant this pool of fish had formed themselves in the fridge and now were on the floor and I had to I mean I got a bunch of them into the toilet and flushed but then there was still this pile of them uh I guess they weren't really moving around although they should have been

There was someone in the bathroom who was mad at me for getting some of this stuff on them but they didn't seem at all scared about the fish anyways I don't know what this dream has to do with the next one which is about being at Renaissance High School and there being uh an invitation for lots of people to come there and there were a lot of you know smart-looking white people dressed nice and business business-like and they didn't understand how the lockers worked and I didn't understand how the lockers worked either because there were two doors

One was a very long door like a locker has and another one was a very short door at the top about 5 inches long and the width of the same door so it was like a little locker inside a big locker but the doors the short door was on the outside. It wasn't at all clear how you were supposed to use the short door to close the locker inside the locker if the big door was in between the inside locker and the out-side locker door but whatever. All you need to know is that it's just like the spout

I was sharing a locker. We were all going to be sharing lockers with the students who seemed to have well the locker who seemed to have very different stuff and young black students at Renaissance had very different stuff than well-off white kids who weren't even kids anymore but who were in their thirties who had been invited to do something professional. They were. We had different stuff. We had different stuff than the black high school students. The student I was sharing a locker with had some little pictures and I guess he seemed like a punk because he had leather cuffs. A lot of black leather. Now it sounds like his locker was a a a little annex for um fuck what was that store called in Royal Oak? Noir Leather. A little annex for Noir Leather. I didn't meet him. We shared the locker but never met. There were little keys to the lockers inside the big lockers. People were wondering how those opened and I'd had an elaborate experience of trying to open my locker. I pretended to know the combination but then realized it was open anyway and I didn't need to pretend I knew the combination and then hope it would open or something cuz that wasn't even the right door. I was traveling through the high school with some of the people that hadn't been there before and I was telling them that I'd been there in the 9th grade and it was Julia that I was with and we walked into a really old part of it and it looked like Renaissance like it was an old church from the inside

We stumbled into a part that looked like an old church and I remember looking out the window and thinking my god it's like we're in the in the DIA like the tower of the DIA that is near all the Jesus stuff and the inside of the Detroit Institute for the Arts that is the café that has the stone walls that are the outside. It was like seeing a prefectory is what I want to say but I'm not sure what that is. It's like seeing a prefectory, a condensation of prefect and factory, but what is that? A prefectory in the distance and seeing that we are also in one and I tell Julia that this part of the school was my favorite part to come to in order to find quiet and there was a display case or some kind of fireplace, a thing that you look at at the head like a pulpit but it was, had glass and there were not necessarily pews but we were there by ourselves at first and the image was like a diorama or a little scene set up behind the glass that, it was one of those scream masks on the head of what was a body dressed like a fascist

And it was a tiny little face or a tiny little version of that scream mask. The mouth wasn't so long um and it was lying on its stomach facing us and so the way you could really see what it was made out of was by looking at it from the side view and seeing that it had these uh boots and bootstraps and a thin leather band around its torso and a little hat that made it look like it was wearing this fascist army uniform um green and it was lying on its stomach with its scream face looking out at us. It was a dummy. It was a mannequin and a kind of artifact as if it existed a long time ago. And then I think Julia or maybe there was someone else there who put on a mask like that. They found one and started pretending to be that guy and I flipped out. I was so fucking serious and I was like do not pretend to be him. That terrifies me. I will kill you. I will freak the fuck out. And I picked up a chair ready to throw it at I think what was Julia who I think was just being funny wearing that mask but as soon as she saw that I was serious she took it off but then there was a man who was a janitor at the school or pretending to be a janitor and he put on the mask and he was not kidding around. He was going to try and hurt us and I picked up an enormously heavy chair and threw it at him but I don't know if it did very much. He grabbed my hand though and I did wrench it free but I saw his eyes and his eyes looked red um through the holes in the mask like he was just taken by so much rage and I think that's me

I think that rage is my feeling because I already have the feeling that I, when I think something bad's going to happen I already have that feeling don't fucking fuck with me I'm going to lose it and you will have no idea what hit you. It's just, it's there in the form of the mask, the masked body the um but it's mine. And it's so Detroit

I have a dream in which another is wearing a mask and I said that it's an artifact and um historical somehow put on display and that's like a dream about aesthetics and it's also a dream about feeling and how you put feelings outside of yourself in order to see them in order to make decorations out of them but also, it makes it possible to disown them to let, to let go of them quote unquote, obviously err not the case, that that is not the way writing and art-making works necessarily uh the mask is you

So you can say that it's a split self and you can say um that we are different people but you know when it comes down to it you are one body with one name and one birthdate and one set of parents and it's like the work of your life to sew those selves together in some way so someone else doesn't take over. So that scream mask um it isn't disassociated from you that if you wanna wear the scream mask that at least you know that it's your desire and not somebody else's don't put it on somebody else cuz nobody's as crazy as you are I mean nobody is your crazy the way you are although there are other people out there that are way more intense

Boomin' Words from Hell

*Boomin' Words from Hell* is the debut album of Esham. It was first released in 1989, when Smith was 13 years old, and was reissued the following year.

*Boomin' Words from Hell* was recorded in one day.

The lyrics of *Boomin' Words from Hell* developed from the turmoil of Detroit at the time, including the era's rise in crack use. According to Smith, "It was all an expression about ['70s-'80s drug cartel] Young Boys Incorporated, Mayor Coleman Young, the city we lived in and just the turmoil that our city was going through at the time. We referred to the streets of Detroit as 'Hell' on that record. So that's where my ideas came from."

*Boomin' Words from Hell* was first issued in 1989. At the time, Smith was 13 years old. It was promoted via word of mouth. Following the album's initial release, the album was reissued with an alternate track listing and artwork in 1990.

According to Smith, the album's lyrical content was so dark that it was the subject of many rumors: "People got the first album, and they would just make up stories. They'd get into an accident and be like, 'I got into an accident because I was playing that tape.' It wasn't like we helped ourselves when we described what was in people's heads. It wasn't to shock people, though, but to get people involved in what we were doing. We had to get people's attention. [...] We said a lot of things that people wanted to say but didn't say. We talked about a lot of political and social [issues] that people didn't want to talk about."

Esham found it difficult to develop a fanbase because many wrote off the dark content of his lyrics and imagery as shock value while hip hop fans did not connect to the album because of Smith's heavy metal influences. In *All Music Guide to Hip-Hop*, Jason Birchmeier writes that "[m]any of the songs here are fairly mediocre relative to Esham's later work, but there are a few gems here that foreshadow his subsequent work." *Rap Reviews* reviewer John-Michael Bond wrote that "the fully realized darkness that surounds both soundtrack and verses on *Boomin' Words*...stands as a stark reminder that just because someone's a kid doesn't mean he can't have anything to say."

We built this gold
We built this gold on

We built this gold
We built this gold on

Built this gold
We built this gold on

We built this gold on this gold
We built this gold on this gold
We built this gold on this gold

Got burnt
Got schooled

We built this gold on this gold
We built this gold on this gold
We built this gold on this gold

Got spent
Got spent

We built this gold on this gold
We built this gold on this gold
We built this gold on this gold

Got
Got

*

Got gilded
Got ghosted
Got the gilded gilt street ghost

Gutted duck
Gristle grape
Seasoned millet

Gore reduction
Glib spit
Pulled gullet

Grazed coon
Honky hip

Breakfast
Spicnic

*

A Way to Start Conducting Business

*(revolver)*
kicks back
loaded

*Guns & Butter*
shoot! the knife!

*Goldfinch American*
plumage rummage
pigeon menu
website says
"picture a Mexican kid
in a grocery cart at a
laundromat"

third world wannabe

*Gold Cash Gold*
green in the filling
chew leisure

*ClandesDine*

*Rubbed*

*Shinola*
I don't know shit from Shinola
But yr clandestinity is too much for me
You made me want to write this plaint
Paint The capital T
Train Station
Across the Street
Black. It
Won't Match
The Gold Sign
Strung From
Slow Leisure
Beam Nostalgic
Klepto
Maniac
Lease Slow
Gilded Image
The Capital T
Train Station
Just
Look
Take It

*Slow's*
Slow Drink
Slow Cure
Slow Sash
Slow Light

Slow Denoument
Slow Diminishment
Slow Devolopeé
Slow Lift
Entrance

Gold Cash Gold
Gold Butter
Gold Gun
Gold (revolver)
Gold Rubbed
Gold Slow
These Gears
Switch Lanes

My Cash
My Watch
My Craft
My Industry
Toss Up My Butter Hair
Color My Main Mane
Disguise Dalliance
And Split My
Name Come
To Slit
My Throat
On the River
Already Dead

Gold Cash
Gold Rubbed
Gold (revolver)
Gold Finch
Gold American
Gold Watch
Gold Who

Gold Me
Gold Bike
Gold Black
Gold You
Gold Tiger
Gold White
Gold Wing
Gold Fist

Deliver Gold
Finch to
American Breakfast

Deliver Gold
Locks to Pinch
This Mess

*Tote Bags around*
*Eyes Instead of*
*Addressing*

Deliver Gold
Tales to Suede
This Hood

Deliver Gold
Watch to Arrest
This Hood

*Tote Bags around*
*Eyes Instead of*
*Addressing*

*

I feel sentimental for
Across the Street
I want to Dine in Glass
Rub it in my hair
Drink a beverage out of it
Cubes of ice look like it
Glass in my lap
On my plate
When I chew it

This wish is
Incident

This building is
Industry Destiny

Donate Skull
Donate Forefinger
Donate Roof of Mouth

*

To build
Or not build

Gild
Or not gild

Built this gold
We built this gold on

Built this gold
We built this gold on

I like Margaritas in Mexicantown
I've had a lot of delicious ones with my friends

I eat BBQ I ride my bicycle
I drink cocktails I ride my bicycle
I drink cocktails I eat pizza I get my haircut
I ride my bicycle I listen to Gil Scott-Heron
I'm singing

And we drink beers and we're Detroiters
And we're Detroiters

*

So about growing up here
So about eating cereal

I ride my bicycle I don't know shit from Shinola
I don't know shit from Shinola

I listen to the radio
Feel the wide stretch of the road

Like to drive
And want to drive fast

This burger is delicious
I love the bacon I love the cheese

When my friends and I in high school used to skip school to smoke
pot sometimes we'd drive around Detroit, sometimes we'd drive
around Belle Isle, sometimes we'd buy weed on the street in Detroit

When I lived in Detroit, I wouldn't drive around Detroit, but I
walked around Detroit and I rode my bicycle a lot

In school. In Detroit. A bus rides on water. Another bus takes a nose-dive, looking dangerous, like it might not resurface. We're required to stay 90 degrees, though another bus dives headfirst into the water. Still. Mostly black girls and a few white ones. Beautiful and sunny out like summer. We're on a big body of water that's not going to freeze. Going 90 miles an hour. Another day. Driving to school. Meanwhile, another white girl. Jogging in front of the car instead of getting out of my way. Ankle fucked up. Walks fast with a limp. Ask her does she want a ride and tells me no. Going to limp the whole way. Really she's gonna skip and doesn't want me to watch. Take a detour. Doesn't matter how I get there. Girls from the Foreign Language Immersion and Cultural School (FLICS) take me to the office. Turn around. Ask a Chinese kid where's the office at and he doesn't know. Because it's his first day. Doesn't care where the office is at anyway. Class is in a room in the hallway. Tell the woman I'm 28. Ph.D. She can't put me in a class with older kids? Didn't need to know all that, she says. Well, okay. But then it's a big deal. Not supposed to say anything. Act normal in high school. Prints a schedule and there's a class about race. I fold the paper. I go to class. People trickle in. In the hallway with lots of chairs. Face the teacher. A chalkboard. Reciting a poem. By heart. Text. Other people. Laugh about a paper. Shows us talking about race. *Singing Anarchy for the UK!* Say "resistance sinks in." Twinkie in mouth. Hawaiian punch washes it down. Try to fill up until same color. All-black. This passage. This passage. Typing teacher's name is Babcock. We make fun of him. The boys like to say cock. Put something on the table. Another piece in front. Wearing a Clockwork Orange t-shirt. Vice-Principal. Vice Squad. Viaduct. Vacation. Vacuum. Volume. Misery. Misfits. Blatz. Bikini Kill. Monster X. Anti-Product. The Murderers. So far up there, we're never coming down unless you take the hooks out. Because we're tired. When we're ready. Our ears. We don't quit. Addicted. Have a body. Can't get rid. Eat candy from kids on the corner. Eat all of it in the car. 8 mile with a dog. Sirens go and Viki smokes, which is the reason she drives with her feet. Trashed from kissing at traffic lights. Drop her. Through the hole of a tire. From so much fun. Is something to watch out for. Being men who give birth. Our descent.

Come and talk to me I really wanna meet you girl I
really wanna know your name
Oh come and talk to me I really wanna meet you girl I
really wanna know your name

You look so sexy you
really turn me on blow
my mind every time I
see your face girl

You look so sexy you
really turn me on blow
my mind every time I
see your face girl

I've been watching you
for so very long
trying to get my nerve built up
to be so strong

I really want to meet you
but I'm kind of scared
cuz you're the kinda lady
with so much class

And the boys that I grew up with
that lived in that neighborhood looked
pretty much like these boys

                  see you lady
I forget what to say
Your eyes

This boy does a good job
at representing
what white boy gangsters looked like in that

neighborhood
um and you know people used to get jumped
or harassed by the police for wearing
certain colors and
red was associated with Latin Counts

I really wanna meet you
Can I talk to you

One afternoon my friend and I walked around
We were babysitting
We were walking around with the baby
in the stroller
all afternoon
following this boy
that we thought was cute and uh
he mooned us at one point he pulled his pants down and showed us
his ass and that made us even more interested in him and we just
kept following him around

I wanna know what it is that makes me feel this way

You know when I lived in this neighborhood and even all the time
that I was growing up in Detroit looking and being looked at were
really powerful experiences um you could get in a lot of trouble for
looking at someone the wrong way and it would feel really bad if
people were staring at you and looking at you look staring at you
looking at you letting you know that you didn't belong by the way
that they looked at you um letting you know that they weren't afraid
of you um it's dangerous it's dangerous that sense of uh taking up
space needing to protect your body and your space but you do that
uh cuz you don't feel uh relaxed you don't feel like it's yours uh the
insistence that this space is yours the insistence that this looking
belongs to you and not to the one that's looking at you that comes
from a place of of not being certain at all that the place that you live

in belongs to you and that the world that you look at um is a place
that you're supposed to be allowed to live in

Oh KC sing to me
said I wanna know you baby

"Street View Lyric" was originally published as a video. I made it using images from
Google Maps of people in my old neighborhood. I was interested in the longing I
felt for people that I did not know, longing I was able to explore because they were
walking streets that were both mine and not mine. Even though Google blurs out
their faces, there are boys and girls who refuse to disappear. There are, for instance,
boys delivering newspapers who see the Google truck and do not turn away from it.
They see the truck later, further on in their route, and they stare at the truck again.
I liked discovering how people photographed by Google had followed the truck with
their eyes. I was grateful for their presence, and their assertion of their presence, in
what are so often represented as abandoned streets, and sometimes are/were, in fact,
abandoned.

If I Had My Way
     If I Had My Way
     I Say Who
     Drop the World
     Break Out

My freshman year of college I was really into Peter, Paul, & Mary. I was also really into Depeche Mode and a bunch of hip-hop and R&B I'd grown up listening to that I was downloading on Napster, like Yo-Yo "You Can't Play With My Yo-Yo" and DRS "Gangsta Lean" and Bloods n' Crips "Piru Love" and Geto Boys "My Mind is Playin' Tricks On Me." I recently thought of Peter, Paul, & Mary "If I Had My Way" though because I thought "if I'd had my way with you, I'd be as happy as I was when I was downloading those songs on Napster." I'd said, "If I had my way, I'd spend nights with you." And this gave me a tingle, like the tiniest but fullest tingle in my clit and in my cunt. So, "if I had my way, I'd spend nights."

But this life is not the Napster of love. I mean, they took Napster away just when it was getting nuts! Just when I was loading up my eMachine—which was this PC version of the iMac, which was the first computer that was all jammed into the monitor, no outside hard drive—just when I was loading up my eMachine with every song I hadn't heard in 4 or 6 years, which seemed lifetimes ago because I was only 18 and I was at the University of Michigan surrounded by wealthy students and all I could think about was how I had grown up in Detroit and these fuckers, they don't know shit—just as I was loading up my eMachine with every song I hadn't heard in years—Ugg boots weren't a thing, but those boys and girls were the same—just as I was loading up my eMachine, we did this horrible thing where everyone stands on a line together and some people step forward and other people step backward and I despised it because it accounted for everything that was explicit and nothing about what had been so obviously fucked. Namely, that I'd spent most of high school high and out of my mind and grieving the loss of my Detroit neighborhood and home, which had been replaced by suburban apartments and townhomes so that I might survive my teens. So, even though I kind of "belonged" at the University of Michigan because both of my parents went to the University of Chicago, briefly—one got kicked out, the other quit to work in a paper cup factory—even though I was white and vaguely well-educated, I had no fucking idea what I was doing there since I'd gone to Detroit Public Schools and grew up with kids with lice in their hair who smelled like pee.

We should have never left Detroit, but also we should have never lived there because my house was the only one I knew of with books and a computer, and my parents, the only ones who talked about "ideas" at the dinner table, if we were at the dinner table, which we weren't because my mom didn't want to feed me and I don't know what my dad was doing. I'd had high hopes of joining the neighborhood female gang Vicious Gangstas and had graffiti all over my bedroom from Cash Flow Posse. Everyone's parents seemed shitty, but with some you could say, they're doing their best and you could forgive them for being exhausted.

So, if I'd had my way, I'd have spent nights with you. Whoever you were. But now I would like to put all that inside a box and shove it, which is to say I wish I could put all this inside a wish and then fuck someone with it. The condensed future of the past belongs to a split. It sticks hard, follows me in the alley. When I crave to be ripped, it's for history to splay out and satisfy not despite but because of this volcano. It is not enough to force my re-emergence instead of seeking a new form, bringing it out to replace the unknown. A form for longing, a form for insurrection, a form for dedication and sacrifice. God. Fuck this invocation. Fuck this protest song. Fuck this religion. "Where have all the flowers gone?" Fuck that. I'll cut into this building so quick, it won't know its split. I set the glass on fire. Cut a head off the headless.

My mom was a communist and really into the idea that the working class would decide who would live and who would die during the revolution. I found nude pictures of her that my father must have taken in a box which I shouldn't have been looking in, but as an only child, often alone in the house, I looked through my parents' things so that they might appear.

In a Kate Bush song, Kate is singing as Peter Reich, Wilhelm Reich's son, the psychologist/ researcher who was hoping to make it rain with an orgone machine. Orgone was a kind of sexual energy that was to be healing and making it rain was supposed to release orgone. The song Kate Bush sings is based on the son's autobiography and we learn of him watching his father being taken away by the government. She says, "I can't hide you from the government . . ." as Pĕter might have. I watched my father get arrested on television during the Detroit Newspaper strike. I saw him grab the ankles of someone else who was getting arrested and get dragged across the television screen. My mother is said to have said, "that's my husband," which is when they arrested her, too. I also heard them tell stories about throwing star nails beneath the tires of trucks and standing around big cans with fires late into the night in the winter.

I first learned about Wilhelm Reich when I started watching lots of Dusan Makavejev films. *WR: Mysteries of the Organism* blew me away. The quote most often pulled out to embody WR comes from the main character, a woman who addresses a crowd of workers from a balcony, imploring: "Communards, fuck freely!" And she is wearing a green hat like people wear in the army and a shirt with a red star and no pants. But somehow I am often less like her and more like my mother's dead baby sister when it comes to freedom.

So, if I had my way, Martha would have learned to jerk off before she died, but I think she was only 10 and I don't think, even if she fucked around with herself, that she could really embrace jerking off, not really, not before 10. So, now that I'm grown, I'd like to jerk off at least once for Martha, and teach her "Juicy Gotcha Krazy" press my warm ass to her cold tombstone, which isn't there because somehow the family failed to mark her grave, so, press my nipples to the grass where her body might be buried, and hope this lovemaking will resolve the pressure exerted on my body when I try to move around.

I wake up thinking, yes. It's a good idea to drive to Minneapolis to see him. I have a dream in which he tells me he's driving this way, will be about an hour away visiting his grandmother and hesitated to say it before, but yes, he would like to see me. He doesn't know if it is the brest idea, but there it is.

I see the typo in his text, which I don't mention, since it's just there, just like that, but there it is.

I wake up thinking my therapist hasn't really been neutral lately, that she's told me men are able to fuck women relatively easily and walk away and women find themselves attached and waiting for men to leave their wives. I say, if I said that in a room full of my colleagues I'd get tomatoed real quick. She says, yes, but your colleagues aren't cultural anthropologists or scientists. This is pretty much fact. Some women can fuck and walk away, most can't.

I remember asking my ex about his past lovers. It must have showed that I was disappointed that he'd never fucked or had a crush on a boy, or I must have just said, I'm disappointed.

I wanted him to be able to say he knew what it was like to be fucked by men. And he did. He just couldn't say it.

In a story called "The Lifted Veil," the person the narrator wants to be with is the person who remains a mystery to him. After he develops both telepathic powers and prophetic insight, no one appeals to him except for the woman whose mind he can't pierce. The lectures the professor gave led to lots of discussion about how love requires mystery, opacity and the game of love is holding some cards close to your chest. I hated this.

I thought they were the worst lectures of the semester since they seemed to say a woman who has no legible mind is the one woman a man who is burdened by his own sadness wants. A man burdened by the knowledge of his own death, his inferiority to his brother, and his inability to please his father—the one woman he desires, the woman he thinks is worthy of his interest, is a woman whose mind remains blocked to him, a woman whose mind frustrates him to some unforeseeable end. This is what he keeps coming back to, his own frustration, his inability to catch her thinking.

And I was just like, well, no wonder I don't love well or am not loved well—well, that's not really true—but no wonder there is no line of suitors for me a la Odysseus' wife or Emily in whatever story because I let it all hang out. And I don't try to frustrate men. I try to please them.

I let it all hang out but not in my body or at least not anymore. I was overweight throughout my twenties because of depression but with a steady Pilates practice over the past 2 plus years and hitting the gym, I'm losing weight and getting ripped. I don't have a flat stomach yet, but I have the line starting below my breasts between my abs, like the 2-pack before the 6-pack.

With my mind, though, I let it all hang out. I wrote a letter to a good friend who I slept with—which was a bad move—but I wrote, "life's too short to pretend certain feelings don't exist." I try to say everything but that doesn't mean I've said enough or if I have, it doesn't mean I've said the things that really matter or if I have, it doesn't mean I've seen what I've said.

Maybe some things really are better left unsaid, but nothing is better left unseen.

It's not just *me* that I think should say everything but I think everyone should say almost everything and wouldn't it be like *What Women Really Want* with Mel Gibson and Helen Hunt where we get glimpses of each other's fantasies, the fantasies that we refuse to share.

Maybe we *do* need protection from each other's insides.

So, I was talking about envy and the shame that comes from it.

There are scenes whose rules I don't understand. I haven't made the rules and when I ask for clarification, nothing is articulated, and I think, if you can't articulate the rules, you don't really have them, and you don't really exist. Then, you toss me about and tell me I'm not the one you love and yet you toss me about and refuse to say the rules while you toss me about and tell me everything.

I have a neighbor who texts me every now and then. He calls me "vecina Anita." I get turned on by this address, which says, hey, neighbor girl, I am close.

There is an assumption of a different kind of closeness that we can play off of like that game we played when we were kids that had all of this anticipation inside of it. It was a kind of game and a kind of ghost story. I'm something something and I'm four doors down. Boom. Boom. And, I'm something something and I'm three doors down. Boom. Boom. And, I'm at your front door. Knock. Knock.

When I jack off, I think of an old teacher, a guy I run into at the coffee shop, my high school boyfriend, exes, scenes from porns. Sometimes my dad pops into my head, but you can't blame me. My mind just does that.

I often think of this scene from a S.I.R. Productions porn where this girl is just going to town on this other girl, I mean her eating her out.

I struggle with this, that the word woman sounds stupid coming out of my mouth and that to talk about fucking, I talk about girls. And to talk about love, I find myself through girlishness.

Do I feel slutty? I feel slutty. Am I ashamed? I'm ashamed. This one time after science class my freshman year of high school, I let this guy suck on my nipple. Another time, during science, while we were in class, I let this same guy stick his hand down my pants. How was it that the science teacher didn't notice? I mean, can you imagine that happening in your class and not noticing? The same guy followed me into the bathroom and I told him to get the fuck out. I'm sure he was confused as, so far, it seemed like I was willing to do anything.

I told a boy in middle school that I loved him after we kissed in the hallway. We were talking on the phone. He was cute. He was tall. He was popular. There was a group of cute boys that hung together: Tim, Derrick, and Antonio. Derrick did something fucked up, but Tim didn't and Tim was my boyfriend. I had lots of boyfriends in middle school and high school.

I was on top of this one guy—not my boyfriend—who was high on heroin and I told him I'd fuck him if he told me he loved me. He wouldn't say it so I just sat there, on top of him, and then we had some kind of fight and he threw his shoe at me and I was really angry and my best friend and I got out of there. And my best friend was like what the fuck were you doing?

This other time, with this other boy I was making out with, that same best friend was like that's not going to go anywhere, don't get hung up on him. And I did and she was like see I told you.

It didn't matter though. There was more where that came from. Someone named Jeff, who was a total jock, not in our social group AT ALL, was into me. My best friend and I hung out with him, went to his jock suburban house with a trampoline in the back. Maybe the word was out that I was a slut. I don't know. I wasn't particularly slutty at that high school though and word couldn't have gotten out to him from that nipple-sucking science boy in Detroit, so maybe Jeff was a good guy.

When I was in the shower I was thinking, how do I become a prostitute. If I wanted to, I don't even know how I'd do that. But at least I'd get paid and the guys looking for fucks, they could just be looking for it, and I could be fucking and getting money and there'd be no pretense of love.

A line runs through my head from that movie where Julia Roberts is crying and yelling at Richard Gere and she keeps saying, "I say who and I say when."

"I say who I say who" and she can't get the lines out because she's so upset. I just keep hearing her say over and over again, "I say who" and her voice cracks at the top of the line, so it sounds more like "I say WHO I say WHO."

I say WHO
I say WHO
I say WHO
I say WHO
I say WHO
I say WHO
I say WHO
I say WHO
I say WHO
I say WHO
I say WHO
I say WHO
I say WHO
I say WHO

And then I wanna turn it into a beat

I say WHO I say when I say WHO
I say WHO I say when I say WHO
I say WHO I say when  I say WHO
I say WHO I say when  I say WHO
I say WHO I say when  I say WHO

But then it goes back to what it was before

I say WHO
I say WHO
I say WHO
I say WHO
I say WHO
I say WHO
I say WHO

And it gets tiresome

I say WHO

I say WHO

I say WHO

I say WHO

I say WHO . . .

She has rules and she sticks by them. The machine of fucking and
money, it seems like it should work great, but Julia Roberts' character
wants to get out of the ghetto and become something and also she
would like to be loved, but men are violent, so, in this scene, all they
know how to do is hit a girl right across the face because, wow, they
teach you how to do that in school like there is a class.

Even though I want to annihilate the world, I pull the world in my direction. The way we are brought close is to be threatened. The world comes, guns ablaze, and the only way I know how to keep it is to pop back. I want to socialize this desire, but the world is not specific, so the list of people I want to destroy becomes just that. It takes up all space.

The logic of the world destroying the world where one figure stands in for itself is not exactly the same as smashing a woman's head by dropping the world on it but it's close.

*I'm gonna pick the world up and I'm gonna drop it on your fuckin head. Bitch,* I say, *you gave birth to me and somehow you remain equivalent to the world outside of which there is nothing. I can't stand you. I see how insoluble this is. I am confused. I am an infant. I could die. Mother, who fucked and then brought me into this world and this world into me, leave earth. Maternal Ground, The Matter of My First Life,* I am saying, *I wish I could skip You.*

My dad was in prison. He was going to be executed. There was a line for loved ones who wanted to talk to prisoners before they were killed. I was at the front of the line using a phone that was supposed to connect us, but I was on hold. I thought I should be crying more. A girl from school was there and had multiple family members in prison. She was trying to comfort me but also needed some comfort for herself, so when she hugged me, her head snuck underneath my chin and she wrapped her whole self around me. We made ourselves look like the right shape for comfort.

D was there, too. He was someone I worked with who I had lots of fantasies about screwing. Also, he stole a lot of money through some very brilliant scheme. And, on slow days, he threw knives at the wall. D walked a line between chaos and control that interested almost everybody at work. I imagine he felt bad about thieving and getting caught; he seemed to carry a lot of remorse in general. When he wasn't being a dick, he spoke softly. People around him felt like he was a gentleman. Carefully combined gentle thug. He was the kind of guy I felt it was important to be liked by even though I thought he was fucked up.

I was listening to this song this morning, Lil Wayne and Eminem's "Drop the World" from the album *Rebirth* in anticipation of going to the gym and letting go of some of my own desires to drop the world or hurl myself against it. I thought of my ex-boyfriend lifting weights like a beast, he'd said, and the potential beast-like qualities of his body, the thick arm with a tattoo of Bukowski's gravestone on it. The tattoo says, *Don't Try*. Does that mean *Don't Try to Live* or *Don't Try to Die*, his ripped chest's hard nipples grazing the wife-beater underneath his hoodie as he hustles on the stationary bike. In the mirror, he groans through a lift. His braid straps his shoulder and he loses himself in his own sound.

*I stare at your ass on the bus. You are wearing jeans that hang off the edge of your tight bubble of an ass and I'm wondering whether you will fuck him just for me. Take this head and make it yours, pulling it in, lifting it up, pushing your tongue down. Make room for my head. Shimmy out of your pants in the farthest corner of the bus to sit on top of my head while the bus heaves uphill. Your tail heavy with fucking, your tail full of my head.*

Eminem raps about fucking the world as a way of dominating it. The desire to master bodies through fucking and by demanding witness to this is contagious. When my ex-boyfriend's mom said fucked up things about me, he threw a television at her on my behalf, or that's how I have tended to think of it, that it was for me. Now it seems they would have also been fighting no matter what and that made me, just partially, the screen being thrown.

*Bitch, I'm gonna pick the world up and I'm gonna drop it on your fuckin head.*

I was pulling the TV, which was on a cart, closer to me from a bed in my dad's study. Instead of moving his shoe, which was on the floor, I pulled the cart over his shoe and the TV came toppling onto my head.

*Bitch, I'm gonna pick the world up and I'm gonna drop it on your fuckin head.*

Pop music gives me—not only me, but I want to own what I take from it—pop music gives me the language to hate my mother and then this hate fans out, to women in general, and this is where the not-me comes in. And maybe it's the other way around. Pop music gives me a song for how much I can hate women and it gives us a scene for seeing how much we can hate our origins.

Tupac asks, *Why do we rape our women, do we hate our women?* He also says, *It's time to be real to our women and if we don't we'll have a race of babies that hate the ladies that make the babies.* He also says, *I was given this world, I didn't make it.* But he did. Or I did. Or we do.

I long for the annihilation of what keeps me hostage, so I can be free, but I am drawn into this orbit, the solar system where the speaker picks up the world and destroys the world and magically remains. This trick demands some behind-the-scenes time veering away from one's own violence and asking women to bear it. I am capable of hating those who are responsible for my birth.

I walk toward the street _____ used to live on. The name of the street should be Grandview, but the green sign gives it a new name and, to make matters worse, the name is in quotation marks. Despite my dream's attempts to re-route, I recognize his house. It is the last one on _____ before the alley.

The house is sky blue with white posts or shutters and a big front lawn. I say "white posts or shutters" because I'm not sure which part is white and I don't know that that matters, but his house has posts and shutters and one of these is definitely white.

A large brick building used to be on the corner of what was now _____, but the place had been knocked down, so next to the alley next to his house, there was an empty lot. Standing on the other side, looking across the busy street through the traffic and onto what was now _____, I see only the side of his house. The blue siding is nothing special except that it belongs to him and, so, me too, since we spend many afternoons listening to Insane Clown Posse in his bedroom.

In real life, it is never possible to see this side from here. In real life, there is a pizza place and a Baskin & Robbins.

In the dream, I stare at the side of his house across the busy street through the traffic at what was now _____ but which used to be Grandview.

_____ was my boyfriend on and off from the fourth to the eighth grade. _____, one of my best friends until the ninth grade, was _____'s cousin. It was _____'s mom that had written the sign "Call Mom" and then, her phone number. It was a sign I'd found while wandering around looking for _____'s house. It was hard to know who it was addressed to and whether the phone number would be right or not: "Mom 313" and then, her phone number. _____'s mom was living in a small place shaped like a pavilion made with lots of glass and wood. I saw her come out and I shouted. It took her a few seconds to recognize me, but as soon as she did, it was like I had never left and she embraced me and welcomed me inside.

_____'s father lived next door, but next door was also inside. In real life, he lived in the house and the garage and also in a small room that was neither part of the house nor part of the garage. I don't know his name, but I feel like it was horrible. I don't know. _____ wasn't my father.

Both _____ and _____'s fathers were abusive. In real life, _____'s father died, not when we were kids, but not long after. And one day _____'s dad chased us all out of the house and her other cousin recorded the whole thing. She said she would use it to prove to the police that he deserved to be in jail. This made him even more angry. I ran down the street and found a pay phone. "Call Mom" and then, her phone number.

This makes at least two fathers that I've known who beat their wives or children or, at least, chased them until they cried. This makes at least two men that I know who hunted their family. Or maybe this makes four.

My dad never hit me. Once, when I refused to go to bed, he got so angry he balled up his fists and his face turned red and he threatened to chase me. I believe he even stomped his foot, which compelled me to charge up the stairs. I feared he was following me.

Another one of these dads was _____. He was the most violent. There were also my neighbors, _____ and _____. I could hear _____ practically torturing _____ in the summer when all our windows were open. But _____ was my childhood friends' father who beat his wife with a hammer so badly that he was charged with attempted murder. He went to jail and the mother changed her name and I never saw her daughters again or at least not until I was an adult and found them on Facebook and drove many miles out to the country to see them. I believe the mother said I looked beautiful.

I felt frightened. "Call Mom."

In the dream, there is a tall man with beautiful colored eyes and a scruffy beard that is part of some sort of scene I am a part of. He asks me what I am doing in the morning and I say I have something at 11 and he says we should do something before then. I don't know what he has in mind, but I agree to meet him. I look up at him with my head craned back and say, "This sounds like a date." I feel childish, so I act it. He touches me a lot and I kind of like it, but I kind of don't. He is too familiar. I remind myself that all men bigger than me will not force me to remember their power.

In the dream, I am in an elevator that is very wobbly and the surface of it is big like it's one of those elevators in museums or at Target. It is open on all sides. I tell a girl to go to the edge because I think we are weighing down one corner and that it might stop wobbling if we even things out. She walks to the edge, but she walks too close, so that when she looks over, she scares herself and she has to run back so quickly that she makes the elevator wobble more. Maybe this elevator is like a wrestling ring and maybe the girl who runs to look over the edge is a version of me running to see if there is anything beyond the ring.

Wrestling runs in my family, but I don't know how to explain that except to say, "_____ was a professional wrestler" and "_____ put his foot on _____'s neck." "Call Mom." I wake up and remember the sign and then, the phone number. "Call Mom" imagines Mom is a name for someone in particular, like anyone would recognize this person as having that name, like anyone could see the sign and understand who to call, as if everyone had the same one and any of us could call, and Mom's number, for everyone, would be "Call Mom" and then, her phone number.

I consider calling _____ _____. _____ is someone who had to find her way through a lot of pain via an early drug addiction, and then, later, like many, a lot of Jesus. So many Facebook posts about

God, I finally blocked her even though she was someone who helped flesh out some of my most sacred experiences of love and joy. I could say the same thing about _____. The first time I ever cut myself I was at her house trying to open a bottle of pop with a knife. I had a crush on her brother and the three of us stayed up all night watching women's wrestling.

_____ was also my sister when we were little and we ate Corn Pops and jumped on the couch while listening to the Pointer Sisters. I own two copies of the Pointer Sisters' album *Break Out*. It's an album with a planet at the center. Blue and purple rays escape the small black hole that is not part of the image but part of the record. The sisters are wearing outfits of nets, lace, beige dangling off them, bunches of fabric, sheer; high pumps, belts, exposed shoulders; looking direct and askant. It's like their outfits are the accessories and the music the clothes. And the songs are love songs, heavily informed by developing technologies.

*Look what you're doing to me,*
*I'm utterly at your whim,*
*all of my defenses down*

*Your camera looks through me*
*with its x-ray vision*
*and all the systems run aground*

*All I can manage to*
*push from my lips is*
*a stream of absurdities*

*Every word I*
*intended to speak winds*
*up locked in a circuitry*

*No way to control*
*it. It's totally automatic*
*whenever you're around*

And then the sister with the bass voice cuts in, further into the chorus, with a deep "automatic," which is particularly catchy because it makes "automatic" sound like an onomatopoeia. "Automatic" comes from the x-ray machine or the camera and every word, like "automatic," is a stream pushing through, from some place completely inside or outside. A stream of absurdities is, one sister says, all she can manage. The problem, then, is that without defenses, our speech is robotic, stuck in a loop beyond control. But that doesn't sound quite right. Love makes me sound like a pop song, absurd because of its automatism. I feel defenseless as a consequence of, say, your presence and when, precisely, absurdity becomes circuitry, well, I can't tell yet.

The sign in the dream says, "Call Mom," and then gives a phone number. Each song here is like a button on a phone and each letter of the sign a name to sing into the mouthpiece of that demand. "Call Mom."

To control love is more violent than the helplessness it demands. "Call Mom."

The tight-knit relationship between music and mom falls out in the glow around my copies of *Break Out*. I jump to other songs that glean love from techne: Kraftwerk's "Computer Love" or Zapp and Roger's "Computer Love" or the Bloods n' Crips "Piru Love." Zapp and Roger's song has a lot of singing, computer-voice singing, but also deep, seemingly collective longing. A pair of voices sings in sync —a masculine and a feminine voice—but also there are two higher voices sometimes or two lower voices. Simply put, there are a lot of different voices in this song and, as it goes on, a desire for dialogue increases but is also echoed, an escalator of kicking back, like having thrown a ball down the steps and watching it misbehave. The sax solo is totally ridiculous but hard not to love because it transforms into keys that resemble (but are clearly not) the sax. The difference in voice is often signaled by a fairy-like electric spark of a scale ascending. This must be the extended remix. The direct address comes in:

*You arrrrre my computer love. Shoo be doo bop shoo be doo bop I wanna love you,* where *I wanna love you* doesn't mean I want to love you and I don't, but I want to make love to you. I want you to let me show you that I love you by spending all night making love with you. You have to let me do this. You have to let yourself be helpless this time, for the time it takes to go from sax to keys, the time the electric-fairy twinkle takes to signal our transition. "Call Mom."

I only learned of Kraftwerk's "Computer Love" when I got to college, and that song begins with loneliness, but Toni and I grew up on Zapp and Roger. We made up the rhythm section with our hands against our chest. We put one hand against our chest and another just a few inches away, so it is suspended mid-air. We use our chest as a bass drum and use the other hand as the snare drum. After doing bass-snare-bass by hitting our chest and then hitting the back of that hand against the hand suspended, and after we hold the bass for a beat longer than we hold the snare, we take both hands off our chest and rub our hands together to make a shuffling sound. We do this 3 times back and forth and then snap to get to the 4. In the Kraftwerk song, the singer doesn't know what to do. He says he needs a rendezvous, but in the Zapp and Roger song, there's already a lover, there's already someone to whom you can sing. I'm not sure which song is dreamier. Even though Kraftwerk starts with a description of loneliness, it's got that great electro-pop that is uplifting, that cruising-down-the-freeway momentum and the German-accented request to *call this number for a data date* that is charming. Its digitality sizzles, is breathy.

These are different dreams. And they are different forms of guilt.

In the Bloods n' Crips' "Piru Love," there is a version of love with death and murder inside. *Every town has an Elm Street but not a Freddy Krueger . . . don't get caught . . .* and then "caught" is rhymed with a stumbling "glah" that ends in "lock." Along the song's waves and its organ hum, a voice belonging to no one sings, *Piru love, baby.* Violence comes to be the background for love, the only way to cry. This is a re-write of "Computer Love." *Shoo be doo bop shoo be doo bop I wanna love you* is buried beneath sorrow. The gang bangers wear doo rags around their heads or mouths. They are men and women making signs with their fingers. *Wrap it around your knuckles, make a fist, and lock it.* The writing that is not on the wall but in the body suggests what could have been but never was. "Call Mom." *Piru is crip in reverse but the c's on its back.* In this song, the "u" is already dead.

Belong
       Belong
       Detroit Dream
       Detroit Detroit

I was with Eminem. Eminem and I were partners. And the reasons we were and should continue to be were obvious. First, we were from Detroit. Second, we were white. But he needed enlightening.

I said to my friend, "I would be so glad to be involved in a poetry reading that brings out some of the black poets on campus because segregation makes me sad." I used the word "sad," but today, it loses meaning. "Sad" is simple, too much without purpose or intention. On the other hand, if happiness is sad's opposite, then between the lines I'd said, "Integration might make me happier at poetry readings."

At least it would be the fulfillment of my dream about Eminem. "But I thought you said you were both white." "For white people from Detroit, like me and Eminem, who want to be there, who want to remain, and by white people, I really mean white children, for children that want to stay where they grow and stay with the people they know, there is a particular sadness when you're asked to become white."

In the dream, I was on top of Marshall. We were fighting, but we were also play-wrestling. It came with the territory that there'd be girls fighting over him and that sometimes he would find it hard to resist them, which was fine. I wasn't mad about that. I was mad because he seemed to think girls were all the same, that we delivered the same things, that we all came to him in more or less the same way, and that, like chess pieces on a board, we had been reduced to types and in this game there were only two types: there was one Queen (him) and many Knights (us). And I was on top of him saying, "Look, lots of women want to care for you, lots of women can give you their bodies, but none of them are going to be like me, and if they are, very few of them will be. So, I've got it all. From the perspective of both the boy in you and the man in you, I got it all. And don't you forget it." And I picked myself up off of him and left him there to stew.

In the dream, I'm talking about bringing someone down who has ascended but has found himself disintegrated by upward mobility. Something akin to how Casey told me when I moved to the suburbs, "You're so white now."

Sure, I looked out for Marshall, kept girls that wanted to fuck him from also stealing the thousands of dollars of cash he kept in his purse. But we went way back. To the extent that we were standing in for each other's pasts, becoming symbols for our childhoods, neither of us were unique. There was hardly anyone around that could perform this for us, and so, in that sense, we were singular. He needed me. He didn't know why and that was his problem.

Our social and cultural lives were so mixed that when we met white people from the suburbs or even sometimes black people in the city who didn't live near white people, those folks thought we were mixed, like actually mixed, because of our behavior. If belonging had a lot to do with race, then we took something in because we were close, or we were taken in because we were close even though neither of us belonged. If something that belonged to black life didn't belong to us, because to say otherwise was to take something from a life that had nothing, well, I guess one thing that this missed was that we never made something from nothing, and the whole story in hip-hop, despite what it says about itself, is about one's inability to come from nothing.

Sometimes a friend or a friend's parents would assert their superiority to black people or Mexicans or Arabs, but this was obviously a mistake because who, then, did they think they were, I mean, who or what did or did they not come from exactly.

Marshall had kind eyes and he was getting over a cold. He wouldn't take Dayquil or anything because he was sober. He dragged his feet as he walked into the kitchen and set down his tea. We talked about what it meant to have these D tattoos, why the D was so hard to shake. Did we even know what the D stood for? And what, in turn, did we stand for? "I don't want to stand for anything," he said. "Me neither. I don't want to be a woman." "I hate myself for being a man. I say so much stupid shit and I don't really feel white, but I know that's what people see when they look at me." "Sometimes I feel like a woman and I hate it. And I dislike being white because it's not supposed to feel like anything, but being poor feels like something." "Being poor feels like shit." "Yeah, but you also feel entitled to claim something invisible like words." "I got this D tattoo because I want to claim the past and, yeah, I feel entitled to it." "But you don't *belong* to the past." "What do you mean by *belong*?" "It sounded good." "So, I don't *belong* to the past? When do I *belong* to then?" "Oh, that sounds better. You belong to when then." "I belong to when then?" "You belong to when then." "I don't know. Does that really make sense though?"

I dream I am in an integrated, all-female rap crew coming out of Cass Technical High School. In the dream I am watching old footage of this integrated, all-female rap crew on youtube. In the dream I say "youtube" and then realize I live in a world where all the technology is for me, but still there are very few, if any, integrated rap crews, and almost no integrated rap crews coming out of Detroit Public Schools.

So this rap crew coming out of Cass Tech. There are three white girls and three black girls. It matters that it is mixed and that all of our hairdos are immaculate. I'm telling this story because what was in place of this was a story about a woman who called me a white bitch after a misunderstanding on the road. It's not important to explain the details of the misunderstanding, only to explain that I wanted to talk about how she called me a "white bitch," but that I also felt and feel like it is fucked up to describe her in this negative way, pointing to her as being a bitch for calling me a bitch, and in this she will also become a so-called black bitch or a brown bitch or, basically, a racialized bitch. It is easy to get drawn into "bitch" and to want to start swinging the term around. What or who does "white bitch" refer to? Myself as victim of misidentification.

Not that I'm not white but that whiteness has now been tied to femininity and a femininity that is not understanding and loving but that is bitchy, that is entitled, that knows too much and has lived too well. If she only knew how much of a bitch I wasn't and had refused to become. If only I could explain that I'd been accepted into the fold, that my dream about the all-female, integrated rap crew, though fictional, recalls being on an all-black cheerleading squad in the eighth grade, where my friends did my hair and I wore the same blue underwear as them, underneath our skirts, so that when we kicked high, we all had the same bottoms on, that we were identical, that that was what cheerleading was about. "We are the Lions and we are the best! We have a team that will put you to the test! We're number 1 and we've just begun. Sit back, relax, cuz we're just having fun!"

It's fair to say that I get called a white bitch because whoever was speaking has already been misidentified and misrecognized so thoroughly that for her to remind me of my race in this strained but telling social accident is one small, momentary way out. I do not want to sideline violence, but I do just want to finish saying what I was saying about the integrated rap crew dream. One girl has pink hair, parted in the middle. Another has a half-pony tail that is high up, with colored stripes. Another girl has barrettes. And another has blonde tips. Hairdos do not always signify girls' skin color. We can want to do each other's hair.

Yesterday, I was writing about cheerleading at Lessenger. I was revising a piece of writing that I've come to call "Detroit Dream" and it's a dream I had about Bobby and Pascal and I added another dream to that that was also a "Detroit Dream," but it was about an all-female integrated rap crew coming out of Cass Tech.

I shook hands with several of the girls after dance class. I told them I was waiting for a train or some other form of transport, that I had to catch a plane, and go home. I'd been doing things on my laptop, taking notes about their dancing, wanting not to forget.

Cheerleading at Lessenger was meaningful. I want to say I was the only white girl even though that wasn't true. For a minute, it was both me and Sandy. Sandy was one of my best friends and we were both on the team until she moved to Ellijay, GA. I had moved and switched schools enough that I had lost all the bodies I belonged to. At Lessenger I could belong to a body that wasn't being forced to move. Even though I am white, I thought, I am on the team. Ebony. Tamara. Chantelle. Kiana. Kiana played basketball and we cheered for her and Andrea and Tosha. Ebony, Tamara, Chantelle, Kiana. I went to the mall with Kiana and we sat in her mother's car and listened to Monica. *Just one of them days, that a girl goes through. When I'm angry inside, don't wanna take it out on you.* There was this white girl who wasn't on any team—I hate to call her that, white, because it feels like punishment—but her name was Tinley. She was mean. She was suffering. She beat the shit out of someone instead of having her pain.

If I was going to stay in my neighborhood I needed to learn to fight, so I fought Dana, this white girl with stringy hair. It seems stupid, but we were fighting over Timothy, the tallest boy, my boyfriend, and we (who was that) felt like Dana posed a threat. It had little do with any of us in particular and some power more generally. I did like I'd seen other girls do. I took off my jewelry and handed it to someone. I have a memory of holding Dana's head and kneeing her in the face. It didn't last long. The permanent injuries we sustained include my shame at something I don't understand and Dana, she found me on Facebook, who remembered the fight and remembered losing. I was afraid more often than not, and so what a show, what a lie. One way to stay in a neighborhood is to make other people feel what it can't.

There was a Detroit, New York. I asked a girl named Anita where she was from and she said Detroit, New York. I told her I was Anita from Detroit, Detroit. I had been wandering around, getting ready to leave. I had a suitcase with a laptop and other kinds of equipment. I'd been staying with a friend and she'd dropped me off. The room was full of people, lots of black men and women dancing in a room with mirrors that were mirrors for them and windows for me. Small, thin, long, thin strips that came down from the ceiling and reached the floor, panels that shifted when you moved, panels that could be turned because they were on a hinge, like a door, except that they weren't doors because you couldn't move through, you couldn't enter and exit through them, although they did provide passage for air and, well, looking, a passage for looking. They were like vents and I could see part of the real dancers' bodies and I could see how I was looking through something that they were looking at. I wasn't clear, it isn't clear, if they would be, if they could also be looking at me as, at, the same time as they were looking at and watching their moves in the mirror. It was clear that they could see me behind the mirror as they were looking at themselves, that our images contained one another. I imagine I was disorienting, but this was the set up: mirrors for them, windows for me, opening like vents and hanging on a hinge that was a string so that our images dangled. And the dancers were sliding across the room, up to the edge of the room, hitting the wall.

I am in a black body suit topped off by white jeans. It is a turtleneck with holes cut out of the shoulders, so it excessively covers my neck and exposes my skin. The contrast between the white of my shoulders and the black of the skin-tight top is perverse like the brightest whitest jeans. A remix of "Thuggish Ruggish Bone" comes on at Lessenger's eighth grade dance and my memory of how I dance is crazy and without form. I am a good dancer, an excellent one really.

Detroit Index
Index

you can't look the other way
you better lose yourself
you are not all that and a bag of chips
wullah i swear to god
Woodward
Wonderland
WJLB
Wigger
who the hell cares
who the fuck are you looking at
Whitlock
where else can i go
when they try to rush
what we'd find
what else is there to do
what else is there to do
what are you lookin' at
Westside
Westland
West Grand Blvd
Waveney
Warren
Warren
Wannabe
walking around
wake up in the morning
Von Bennett
Virginia Claxton
Victor Sandecki
Vicious Gangstas
Vernor's
Two-Faced
Two thousand and two
Two thousand and twelve
Two thousand and three
Two thousand and thirteen

Two thousand and ten
Two thousand and sixteen
Two thousand and six
Two thousand and seventeen
Two thousand and seven
Two thousand and one
Two thousand and nine
Two thousand and fourteen
Two thousand and four
Two thousand and five
Two thousand and fifteen
Two thousand and eleven
Two thousand and eight
Two thousand
Truancy Officer
Triflin'
Tosha Diggs
Tony
Toni Tuminello
to feel that touch from your hand
to be me
Tiombe
time to heal
Thug
through each other's eyes
Three one three three three six two one two one
Three one three three three seven eight two eight two
Three one three five eight four six four nine five
Three one three five eight four six five five seven
Three one three five eight four nine two three seven
Three one three
things won't be the same
things will never be the same
things will never be the same
they got a war on drugs
they can all get fucked

they can all get fucked
there's war in the streets
the Train Station
the Southfield
the Rouge
the River
the Quiet Storm
the penitentiary is back
the Lodge
the Hudson Building
the Fox
the DPL
the DIA
the Box
the Big Three
the Belcrest
that's what Huey said
that's the way it is
that's the sound of my 2
that's just the way it is
that's just the way it is
that's just the way it is
that's just the way it is
Terry Cross-Nelson
Terry
Tamara Dawson
take the evil
sweet fantasy
streetlights people
straight slangin'
Stout
still i see no changes
step back
stealing weed
stay in your place
standing on the corner

Stahelin
St. Mary's
Southwest
Southland
some will win
some will lose
some things will never change
some punk that i roughed up
so the police can bother me
so i'll cry for you
smoking weed out of a pop can
smoking weed out of a pop bottle
smokin' crack
smokin' blunt after blunt
Slut
Skank
sitting on the porch
Simone
Shylah-Beth
Shovel
should i blast myself
Sherrie
Shelley
Shawn
Shaun
Sarah Stark
Sandy Johnson
Sam
Rutland
Rutherford
Ruddiman
Rosie
Rosemont
Rollerdrome
Rob Sandecki
RK

Ricky Rodriguez
Ricky Johnson
Ricky
rest in peace
Renaissance
Remy
Redford
rat tat tat tat tat
Randell
racist faces
Quinyl
Quinn
Qiana
pussy ain't got no face
Punk Bitch
pull a trigger
pimp smack you up
Pig's Feet
Piedmont
Phil
Pershing
Penrod
Peaches
Party Store
Outer Drive
one less hungry mouth
one day soon we'll be hangin' out
one day i'll be in the dirt
now slide just slide
Northland
Ninety-six point three
Ninety-seven point nine
Nineteen ninety-two
Nineteen ninety-three
Nineteen ninety-six
Nineteen ninety-seven

Nineteen ninety-one
Nineteen ninety-nine
Nineteen ninety-four
Nineteen ninety-five
Nineteen ninety-eight
Nineteen ninety
Nineteen eighty-two
Nineteen eighty-three
Nineteen eighty-six
Nineteen eighty-seven
Nineteen eighty-one
Nineteen eighty-nine
Nineteen eighty-four
Nineteen eighty-five
Nineteen eighty-eight
Nikki
never seen a man cry
my stomach hurts
my momma didn't raise no fool
my mind is always with you
Mumford
Monkey
misplaced hate
Minock
microwaving weed in the lady's we babysat for microwave
Michael
Mexicantown
Metattal
Mercy
Memorial
McKenzie
Mauricio
Mary Ann Johnson
Mary
Mario
Malice Green

makes disgrace
make a bowl out of a pop can
make a bong out of a pop bottle
Mack
Lyndsey
losing all my muthafuckin' friends
look at shit
Livernois
Lisa Johnson
Lindsay
let's trade shoes
let me hear you say
Lessenger
learn to see me as a brother
learn a lesson
Laymon
Latin Counts
Lafayette Park
lady what do i do
lady i will cry for you tonight
lady i will cry for you tonight
lady i will cry for you tonight
lady i will cry for you tonight
Kylie
Kristine
Kim
Kiana
Khaleed
Kerry
Kerry
Kensington
Kenny
Kelley Williams
Kathy
Karen
Justin

just to see what it's like
just to see what it'd be like to
just to see
just stay true to you
just stay true to you
just a city boy
Junior Kubiak
Joy Rd
Josh
Jeremiah
Jefferson
Jay Warren
Jason
James
James
Jake
it's on us
it's hard to be optimistic
it's been an hour since you've been gone
it's amazing whatcha do
it takes skill to be real
is life worth living
instead of two distant strangers
instead of a war on poverty
Inkster
i'm tired of being poor
i'm reaching out for you
i'm losing my fucking mind
i'm living on the edge
i'll knock your eyes outside your head
i'll be you
i'll be one tough act to follow one tough act to follow
i'll be one tough act to follow
i'd love to go back to where we played as kids
i would do anything for you
i would do anything

i wonder what it takes
i wish i coulda been another
i was just in your neck of the woods
i see no changes
i see no changes
i say you're everything i do
i made a g today
i know it seems heaven sent
i gotta stay strapped
i gotta get paid
i got love for my brother
i feel worthless
i feel for you
i ended up in this position i'm in
i don't trust this
i don't know i don't know
i don't know i don't know
i don't know how why or when
i don't give a damn anymore
i can't think without you
i can't live without you
i bust this
Hussy
how long will they mourn my brother
How Long Will They Mourn Me
how can the devil take a brother
Hostess Cupcakes
Honky
Honey Love
Hoe-bag
Hoe
hey that's the way it is
Hemlock
Hart Plaza
Harper
Greenview

Gratiot
Grandville
Grandmont
got a problem
go inside
GM
give 'em guns
get on my knees for you
get on my knees for you
Gardner
Garden City
Gang Squad
from my heart to the trigger
Frank Stark
Four eight two two four
Four eight two two eight
Four eight two three seven
Four eight two three eight
Four eight two one seven
Foreign Language Immersion and Cultural School
Fordson
Ford Woods
Ford
For the Love of Money
Folk
Flaming Hot Cheetos
Five point oh
Five four three two one, come on now
first ship 'em dope
Finney
feel your pain
Faygo
Fairlane
every muthafuckin' day
Evergreen
Erika Miskovitch

Erica O'Brien
Eric Sajewski
Eastside
Eastland
Downtown
don't roll your eyes
don't let 'em say you ain't beautiful
don't let 'em say you ain't beautiful
don't let 'em jack you up
does anyone know what i'm talkin' about
do what you want me to
do what you want me to
do anything that i can
Dinty Moore
didn't realize how much the little baby had her eyes
Diane
Diane
diamond in the back
Devon
Devil's Night
Desmond
Derrick
Dearborn Heights
Dearborn
Dayton
David
Dairy Queen
crack you up
cops give a damn
comin' back after all these years
come on back
come on back
Cody
Cobras
Cobo Hall
Clayton

Cindy
Chucky
Chrysler
Chris
Chantelle
Chadsey
Cassie
Cash Flow Posse
Casey
Carver
Carmen
Carl
Candice
Cadieux
but you made it
but we can never go no where
but things change
but now i'm back with the facts
but i'll cry
but i'll cry
Burton
Brian
Bri Williams
Brandon Cardillo
Bobby Vandevender
Bobby Jastren
Bob Johnson
Big Sonic Heaven
Bettermade
Belle Isle
bein' real
Beeper
Bates
Basics
Banquet
baby i'm beggin' beggin' baby

baby i'm beggin' beggin' baby
baby i'm beggin'
baby i'm beggin'
Auburn
Ashton
Ashley Johnson
Ashley
Ashley
Asbury Park
Artesian
are you tryin' to get through
are you reaching out
are you calling me
Archdale
April
Antonio
Anthony
Ann Arbor Trail
Angie Hernandez
Andrea
and that's too long
and that's the way it is
and that's how it's supposed to be
and it's filled with blacks
and i never get to lay back
and even worse i'm black
and ask myself
and as long as i stay black
Amanda
all i see is
Alison
Alex
ain't worth a foodstamp
ain't 2 proud 2 beg
about the payback

Detroit Birthmarks
Birthmarks

It's at the center of my face. I feel it when I touch my nose. I feel it when I watch someone touch their nose after looking at me. I don't know if they're afraid that a birthmark has suddenly surfaced as a result of looking at me. Or maybe it's a coincidence.

My birthmark was small, dark red or deep purple, called a port-wine stain. Or maybe it's a hemangioma. The laser surgery was supposed to make it lighter. Something akin to leaving your most colorful shirt in the back seat of your car for weeks, even months, and then coming back to find that it's faded unevenly from baking in the sun and it looks kind of pathetic. Except I wake up in a hospital in San Francisco, holding an ice pack against my nose. My face hurts. It's too hot and it's too cold. I feel cut. I am lying on my side in a big ugly white room.

*I sit alone in a four-cornered room staring at candles. Oh that shit is on. Let me drop some shit like this here, real smooth.* This is how the rapper Scarface clears his throat at the start of "My Mind is Playin' Tricks on Me." I keep the memory of the Geto Boys's most popular song close. July 1, 1991. "My Mind . . ." was released one day before my 10th birthday and several years after the surgery on my birthmark.

The Geto Boys's song samples the fantastically catchy Isaac Hayes cut, "Hung Up On My Baby," from the *Three Tough Guys* soundtrack. The riff that opens Hayes's song is almost bubbly in its mystical, twinkly funk. It's cushy and smooth, but in the Geto Boys's hands, the opening is less clean. We don't hear the entry of alert horns or a finely tuned ascent. The translation of something like 70s spirituality into 80s and 90s anxiety brings an unmistakable fog.

"My Mind is Playin' Tricks on Me" preserves the static of Hayes's vinyl. Or, we're meant to imagine that this static is original to the sample they're using, but when I listen to the Hayes, I don't hear the static. I think it's something the Geto Boys and their producers added to make the sample sound authentic. Instead of a song that's about to get off the ground, the warm crackle at the start of "My Mind . . ." makes it sound like the record was skipping before it even started.

After the surgery, I kept doing things to interfere with healing. I was rolling a television on a cart over a shoe and wound up with the TV on my face. My lip split open. I fell off a trampoline. More scars were on my birthmark now than before. The surgery was supposed to make the mark less visible. It was also meant to reduce the excess of bloody noses that I had been having. But the surgery made everything more palpable to me. And I seemed, unconsciously, to want to bring the mark's scars to the surface.

It takes a moment for Scarface to realize that they're already recording "My Mind . . ." When he does, the jam really kicks in. We hear a muddy-sounding, deep thump underneath his confession. *At night, I can't sleep. I toss and turn. Candlesticks in the dark, visions of bodies bein' burned.* The song tracks the feeling of falling in and out of sleep, coming in and out of the most obfuscated places. It also imagines being burned in the dark.

It is hard now not to think of the beginning of *The Autobiography of Malcolm X*, where, in his mother's womb, Malcolm Little is witness to Klansmen coming to his house, yelling at his father with torches in their hands. But as a child, I associated to my own vision, my birthmark. So, when Scarface sings of "visions of bodies bein' burned," I think of my six-year-old face being burned to make something dark light. And I spend years identifying with Scarface for reasons I can't completely explain.

I live in Detroit, go to Detroit Public Schools, and have something on my body that I can't wash off. I am white, but not white like kids in the suburbs. My birthmark, which hardly feels like mine—I mean what have I done to own it?—causes both horror and fascination, rejection and curiosity. A boy tells me I have marker on my face. Someone else suggests it's bike grease. Someone else asks if I got a tattoo. Someone else, if I've had a septum ring gone wrong. Other people simply say, what happened to your nose? I respond, it's a birthmark. Or, I was born this way. They apologize for asking, being curious, or being rude. I don't want them to feel bad for making me feel bad, so I try to assuage their guilt, the coincidence of curiosity and ignorance, their inability to help themselves. They just can't help but ask. But they didn't mean to hurt me, right? None of us really mean to hurt, do we?

One time I nicked my birthmark with a pen cap that I'd been chewing on. It bled for hours. I mean it was bleeding for 3 whole hours. I had to sit or lay with my head back, blood running back into my nose and throat, pressing on the front of my face with wet tissue or cloth. Scarface tells us about how sleepless nights are charged by nightmares. *Every time my eyes close, I start sweatin' and blood starts comin' out my nose.* He tells us about how hard it is to distinguish between what we see in our mind and what we feel in our body and how scary that confusion can be. In "My Mind . . ." one of the other Geto Boys recounts a time when he discovers himself beating up a shadow. Someone was following him, but then, he says, *My hands were all bloody from punchin' on the concrete.* And then, the refrain, *It's fucked up when your mind is playin' tricks on you.*

These lyrics belong to what has been dubbed one of the best rap songs of all time. This says something important about our collective taste for rap music and what it's been giving us all these years. But what does this taste tell us?

I am pretty sure the first time I heard "My Mind . . ." was on The Box. The Box, first called the Video Jukebox Network, was a TV channel started in Miami, FL. Sometimes The Box only displayed a list of songs with codes and the 1-900 number that you should call to make a video request. Who knew how long it would take for your request to come up or how long it would be until another video played? I can remember the one time I actually called the number. Me and Casey called to request a Marilyn Manson video from the lady-that-we-baby -sat-for's house. It was their cover of the Eurythmics's song that goes, *sweet dreams are made of these.* Whenever the video came on, whatever video it was, it was like being in that dark room Scarface is rapping about, a dark room with a few candles and scary but gripping dreams.

The Box was part of the emergence of Miami Bass music, whose heart was the deep bass of the 808 drum machine. These songs' fast tempos and electro-fires pushed dancing into more-than-dancing. They asked you to be in the beat. Groups like 2 Live Crew and Poison Clan brought that excess into their lyrics. With songs like "Me so Horny," "Pop that Coochie," and "Shake What Ya Mama Gave Yaa," the beats and the dancing spilled what couldn't be contained for listeners to sip up through a straw. But it was far too much, and it was horribly mixed up with a view of black men and women's sexuality as being impossible to control. But for kids with nothing else to do but be in the basement, walk the streets, listen to the radio, and make up dance routines, the music was difficult to ignore and hard to resist.

I learned about Oaktown's 357 from The Box. A female rap group produced by MC Hammer, their songs, if they were played on the radio, were the ones being played at 3 in the morning. I watched their video to the weirdly drowsy dance song, "Yeah Yeah Yeah," which makes a lot out of the chorus, *Yeah yeah yeah yeah, yeah, yeah, oh yeah*, and carries a quiet MC-Hammeresque *here we go, here we go* chant in the background. This is like Billie Holiday's *Ooooooo what a little moonlight can doooo*, where the content is in the repetition of similar sounds and not so much in the words themselves. To my little girl ears, The Box wasn't just ahead of the curve—The Box was the curve.

I got Oaktown's 357's tape and my friend Andrea and I found neon-colored sports bras and tight shorts to imitate them in our own debut. We choreographed a dance to their "We Like It (Git Loose)" and performed it in the auditorium at Carver Elementary. *3-5-7 get loose!* The song offers a different kind of countdown: one that says, *weapon* and *dance* in the same breath. Oaktown's 357's name refers to a .357 Magnum.

Only as an adult did I realize that my favorite song by Oaktown's 357, "Juicy Gotcha Krazy," was about how women's bodies (our "juice" in particular) might cause men to become addicted to us. Oaktown's 357's weird feminist anthem was something I embraced without quite knowing what its story was. I knew that I might want this juice to belong to me. I wanted to be part of something and these women rapping about their juice in a convertible in California seemed (and still seems) the way to go. Several years ago, I spent hours transcribing the words to "Juicy Gotcha Krazy" because the internet was incomprehensibly lacking the lyrics to this gem. *Fly girls get served cuz the juice is so prime.* And I dreamed of being a Fly Girl on the TV show "In Living Color." How could I not want to be fly? How could I not want to be served? Even if I didn't know what that was exactly?

The images of black women on The Box were contradictory from the start. Yo-Yo was warning men, *You can't play with my yo-yo*, which I thoroughly admired, especially because she was chewing out her listener for not knowing their *week was Monday through Sunday*, and also, by the way, *the earrings* she wears *are called dolphins*. In her most well-known song, "You Can't Play with My Yo-yo," Yo-Yo was taking names and laying down the law about what was what. *I rock the mic, they say I'm not lady-like, but I'm a lady.* I wanted to be lady-like in the way that she was not lady-like. I wanted to get loose like Oaktown's 357 and be part of the U.N.I.T.Y. that Queen Latifah was rapping about.

In the basement of my house on Longacre on the west side of Detroit, I grew attached to what existed for me to consume. These songs and rappers often felt more real than the nothing that the city bore at large. So, like many other kids, I developed an attachment to representations of black men mostly rapping about violence, fear, the horror of their lives and their streets. I became attached to stories where black women talk about being women, sexuality, and defending themselves. Much of the time women were dancing for men, sure, but a lot of the time they were also dancing for themselves and each other. TLC's "What About Your Friends" is a visceral rap song about loyalty and our ability to stick together, given the violent impulses that might erupt between us. Left-Eye raps about self-hate in that song. Not to mention SWV, En Vogue, Xscape, J.J. Fad, even in the video that Janet Jackson and Paula Abdul did together for "Nasty Boys"—they were all getting into something that wasn't just for show but was about being a group, having a crew, watching each other's backs. They pulled it all together with fresh moves and tight lyrics. As far as I knew, I could be part of this world, too. And, in a way, I already was.

It was hard to feel different than what I saw. I mean both that I felt different but also that it was impossible to always feel that way. Sometimes I wanted to and sometimes I didn't, but I'm not sure when it was a choice. To my kid mind, Detroit seemed like Compton or Brooklyn or Miami or wherever there were lots of black artists and I was part of the bodies in those cities, too. These distinctions were often more salient, more palpable to me, than not being black. Except when they weren't. My neighborhood was mostly white and my schools were mixed or mostly black. Until I was 18, I'd had just as many black and brown boyfriends as I'd had white, but the only time I went into the projects, Herman Gardens, which were 2 blocks away, was to look for a bike that my friend's mom was certain had been stolen and then the thief they'd imagined, surely black, had absconded to the projects. We drove around looking for the bike. Now Herman Gardens is gone and the middle school next door, Ruddiman, is closed. Race wasn't precisely the way I could divide my life and its relations, but it was never not there. In fact, I had no idea what it meant except that it was one of the most powerful social forces shaping me, both pulling and pushing, including and excluding.

In college, I made a t-shirt for a performance art class which read, "what happened to your nose? what happened to your nose? what happened to your nose? what happened?" It was in pink letters, imperfectly screen printed on a white shirt whose sleeves I'd cut off. I wore it for one day, which wasn't long enough. Now I have a tattoo on my arm, which is only visible if I'm wearing a sleeveless shirt, that reads "Detroit Detroit." Except that the second time the word appears its written in its mirror image. It takes people a minute to realize that the word is there twice because its second appearance is only immediately legible in a mirror. It's a tattoo about legibility, about reading "what happened" to my body in relationship to where I came from, including the other bodies that made me. It's about geography and difference and being born after the record has already started to skip.

I struggle with identifying a difference between what I was looking at on the screen, what I saw or heard about in my neighborhood, what I'd seen on my own face, and all the other people I knew. I never forgot that I was white, which is a unique experience for white folks. I was called "honky" in the 3rd grade. In the ninth grade, Bri Williams called me her "nigga." Even as an adult, I've been told I'm one of the blackest white people so-and-so has ever met. I mean my friend whose mom is white and whose dad is black feels this, I think. But what's it mean? It is something I feel proud of sometimes, why not? But it's not exactly a confusion that I sought out, nor is it something I know how to move around, and it doesn't make sense to pretend otherwise. I don't even know what otherwise would be. I was a product of living in a place whose scars were on the surface and I found myself with a face that participated in that conversation unbeknownst to me. It is a conversation is what I want to say. *Come and talk to me I really wanna meet you girl I really wanna know your name.*

Also, there was nothing else. There was nothing good about living in Detroit except for the music and the dancing and the people I shared it with. The music on The Box and on FM 98 WJLB was mostly black. It was primarily made by, spoken by, and hosted by black people, and this is what told me and my friends about our world. And, as the city changes, I continue to identify with Detroiters, who remain mostly black, as national and international taste for the city changes, yet seems to have little to do with what some of the kids who grew up there remain attached to, confused by, held by, and not letting go of.

I went to Renaissance High School for one year and after that we left the city. The cheer for the high school went, *R-E-N-A-I-S-S-A-N-C-E, oh yes, we are the best.* It was paced in such a way that "S-S" rhymed with "the best." This is the way I remember how to spell "renaissance." But the pressure around difference, the confusion of belonging, was tripping me out. Somehow, I thought I'd be happier if we lived in the suburbs. As soon as I got there, I knew I was wrong. I'd never seen so many white people in one place in my life. I was horrified. Again, I knew I was white, but I was *never* going to be *suburban* white. That was a whole new class of white. *That* was *really* white. I made myself as different as possible. I got dreadlocks. I got called dirt-ass. I got suspended.

The doctors are going to put me to sleep. They ask me what cartoons I like. I say, the Smurfs. Then they ask me to name all of them. When I imagine myself on the operating table, looking up at the mask as it looms over my face, coming in closer to cover my nose and my mouth, I can't think of the names of the Smurfs. Instead, I think of Gargomyl and the Seven Dwarfs. I don't want to think of the Smurfs' cuteness or the attending beauty of Snow White. I want what feels like the ugly name, even the evil one, and I want an entourage of people like me to protect me. But what is like me? Who is like me? Do we even exist?

I am thinking of the song "Miami's Rockin' Baby (Miami Jams)." Two sentences crunched together, the name of the song brings home the density of Miami Bass and the complexity of my love for that music and Detroit. *Miami's rockin' baby. Miami jams.* To my ears this means: cars with big speakers in the trunk and music made for those speakers, music made for the bass of it and nothing else. This can feel like pure sound, living for the bass, except that there is so much tied up with bass, the trunk, the beat, speakers, rocking, babies, and jams. It's hardly simple.

On Warren Avenue, there was a rollerskating rink called the Roller-drome. They had pizza at the snack bar that tasted like the cardboard it was frozen on. They had a payphone in the back on which groups of girls made mean phone calls. I made those calls and received those calls. They involved threats to come over and kick somebody's ass, talk of who said what about who because she had heard that you were talking shit and why weren't you there if you didn't have anything to hide? Rumor had it that some gang members were kicked out of the Rollerdrome and they came back and burned it down. For sure, it was there one day and gone the next. RIP Rollerdrome. Rollerdrome Love.

In my neighborhood, gang bangers—I wanted to be in a gang when I was twelve—used to say "Cash Flow Love" or "Latin Count Love" and "Family Love." We would yell at cars as they passed saying which gang we were a part of (or wanted to be a part of) and we'd follow it with the word "love." We'd do this with our own names, too. My best friend Sandy had a gang name. I don't remember what it was, but let's say it was Angel. She would say "Angel Love" as a way to represent herself. I would say "Peaches Love" as a way to represent myself. I have no idea how I came up with Peaches. Surely, it was in the air.

One of my favorite songs to skate to was a song that makes you feel like you can rollerskate no matter what kind of shoes you're wearing. It's Afrika Bambaataa's "Planet Rock." This song *is* outerspace, a version of Miami Bass which builds a rocket to the moon that promises to take you home. It riffs off Kraftwerk's "Trans Euro Express" but, of course, to a lot of us it feels like Kraftwerk is pulling from "Planet Rock" because our access to Afrika Bambaataa and the Soulsonic Force preceded our knowledge of the German electro group. And didn't Detroit make the ground for that electro anyway? What's the beginning? And what's before that?

Afrika Bambaataa played at the big electronic music festival in Detroit several years ago. At first the festival was called DEMF, The Detroit Electronic Music Festival and it was free, *absolutely free.* And this blew everyone's mind and it was like a dream come true. And then it was called Movement and maybe it was still free but it seemed different and now it's not free. Anyway, I watched Afrika Bambaataa sing "Planet Rock" with the Detroit River behind him on a summer day. *The Soulsonic Force, it's the big pow wow,* and I was levitating, filled with a sense of belonging to a past and to a possible future. The bass and the beat demanded it. Is this joy the other side of the scar? Could we not skate free if we hadn't marked the scar in the first place?

I used to come home with a blister the size and shape of a fat worm on one foot. We went in the same direction for most of the night and so there was always pressure on that one heel as I swerved around the corner. Being on rollerskates was like being in a car with the windows rolled down. I felt free, in charge of my body. There was air moving around me and the music was on. They had a time for couples to skate, a time to skate backwards, and a time to funk-skate, which meant dragging one skate in, behind the other, to make a slide to the left and a slide to the right. They switched things up so you had to skate in the other direction. *We are lost in a storm, don't know what to do, been around the world in a day.* I misheard the lyrics to Chubb Rock's hazy tune, which got us swirling around the rink like we were at the center of a tornado, mildly under our control. I thought the song said, *been around the world in a daze.*

Scars that stay on the surface: I have a taste for this. At the same time, these scars are not only themselves. Just like the start of the Geto Boys's "My Mind . . .," I add static to the sample to make it sound authentic. I draw on the raw before the raw, the grime before the dirt, the skip before the start, and I come by this desire honestly. What else could I want? *Uh uh.*

The cultural representations that I am attached to are not necessarily more or less real than other attachments, but they are some of the most enduring and difficult to decipher. Lil Wayne raps in "Drop the World," *Confidence is a stain you cain't wipe off.* I'm sure he's talking about blackness. There are some things that you're born with that you also make. And there are some things you're born with that do not belong to you.

Today I understand how, even as a kid in Detroit, I was protected by whiteness and having parents who were well-educated. But, for the most part, none of us felt protected by anything. So, when I watched Tupac's reportage in the music video to "Brenda's Got a Baby" about a twelve-year-old girl who has a baby on the bathroom floor and then becomes a murdered prostitute at the end of the song, it seemed like it could be my public school's bathroom, some friend of mine in the future, my baby in a dumpster, or even me, because as a life we were so unclear.